The History of the Television

Elizabeth Raum

Heinemann
LIBRARY

www.heinemann.co.uk/library
Visit our website to find out more information about Heinemann Library books.

To order:
 Phone 44 (0)1865 888066
 Send a fax to 44 (0)1865 314091
 Visit the Heinemann Bookshop at www.heinemann.co.uk/library to browse our catalogue and order online.

First published in Great Britain by Heinemann Library,
Halley Court, Jordan Hill, Oxford OX2 8EJ, part of
Pearson Education.
Heinemann is a registered trademark
of Pearson Education Ltd.

© Pearson Education Ltd 2008
First published in paperback in 2009
The moral right of the proprietor has been asserted.

Editorial: Kristen Truhlar and Diyan Leake
Design: Victoria Bevan and Tower Designs Ltd
Picture research: Mica Brancic
Production: Julie Carter

Origination: Dot Gradations
Printed and bound in China by South China
Printing Co. Ltd

ISBN 978 0 431 19150 8 (hardback)
12 11 10 09 08
10 9 8 7 6 5 4 3 2

ISBN 978 0 431 19156 0 (paperback)
13 12 11 10 09
10 9 8 7 6 5 4 3 2 1

British Library Cataloguing in Publication Data
Raum, Elizabeth
The history of the television. - (Inventions that changed
the world)
1. Television - History - Juvenile literature 2. Television
- Social aspects - Juvenile literature
I. Title
303.4'833
ISBN-13: 9780431191508

Acknowledgements
The publishers would like to thank the following for
permission to reproduce photographs: p. **4** akg-images, p. **5**
Science & Society/NMPFT/Daily Herald Archive, p. **6** Science
Photo Library, p. **7** History of Advertising Trust, p. **8** Corbis, p.
9 Getty Images/American Stock, p. **10** Corbis/Bettman, p. **11**
Corbis/Bettman, p. **12** Corbis/Bettman, p. **13** Camera Press/TLB,
p. **14** Getty Images/AFP, p. **15** Topfoto, p. **16** Photolibrary.com,
p. **17** Corbis/Russell Underwood, p. **18** Mary Evans Picture
Library, p. **19** Corbis/Stockbyte, p. **20** Topfoto/Image Works, p.
21 Art Directors/Ark Religion, p. **22** Corbis/Jose Luis Pelaez,
Inc., p. **23** Alamy/Huw Jones, p. **24** Getty Images/Tim Boyle, p. **25**
Getty Images/Stone/Flying Colours, p. **26** Rex Features/Heikki
Saukkomaa, p. **27** Corbis/Jose Luis Pelaez, Inc.

Cover photograph of a boy watching sports on a
General Electric television receiver reproduced with
permission of Corbis/Hall of Electrical History Foundation/
Schenectady Museum.

Contents

Some words are shown in bold, **like this**. You can find out what they mean by looking in the glossary.

Before television

Before television (also called TV), people went to the **theatre** to see films and plays. In the evening, they read books and newspapers. People also listened to the radio.

Long ago, people only got the news from newspapers.

Before television, families listened to the radio together.

People liked to hear music on the radio. The radio also had news and sports **programmes**. Children listened to storytellers on the radio.

The first television

In 1924 John Logie Baird, of Scotland, was the first person to **invent** a television that worked. Baird's television was very big. The first picture was fuzzy.

This photo shows John Logie Baird with one of his first televisions. It looked very different from televisions today.

Baird showed his television to people in Selfridge's.

Baird tried to get people interested in his television. In 1925 he put a television in a department store in London called Selfridge's. Hundreds of people watched Baird's television in the store.

Moving ahead

John Logie Baird wasn't the only **inventor** working on making a television. In the United States, Charles Francis Jenkins also made a television. In 1925 he was able to show moving pictures of a windmill over his television.

This is a photo of Charles Francis Jenkins watching his television.

The first television
screens were small.

The first televisions did not have sound or colour. They showed fuzzy black-and-white pictures. Some televisions were big, but the picture screens were small. Inventors wanted to make television better.

Making television better

In 1927 an **inventor** in the United States named Philo T. Farnsworth made a new kind of television. His television was different from other televisions. It was called an **electronic** television because it used electricity.

Philo T. Farnsworth showed his television to many people.

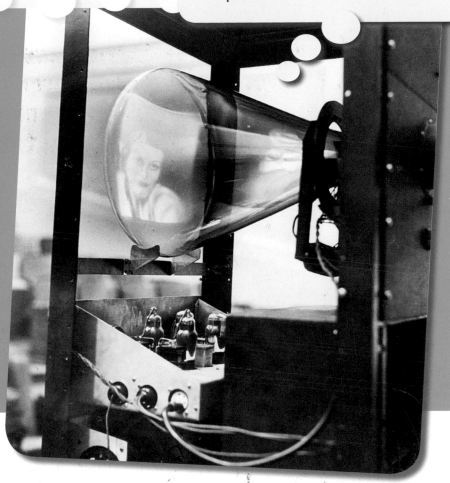

This picture tube shows a picture of a woman's face.

Farnsworth's television used a picture tube. The picture tube was made of glass. Televisions that look like a box still use picture tubes. Farnsworth worked for 10 years to make his television even better.

People want to see TV

The first television shows began in 1928 in the United States. Televisions cost a lot of money, so very few people owned them. In the United Kingdom, the first **programmes** began in 1929. At first they were only on at night.

This was one of the first television shows.

Many people watched television for the first time in 1953 when Queen Elizabeth II was crowned.

Soon television programmes were on more often. Store owners put televisions in the windows of their stores. People enjoyed watching television. By 1945 many people were buying televisions to watch at home.

Colour television

The first television **programmes** were only in black and white. At the cinema, people could watch films that were in colour. People also wanted to watch television shows in colour.

Millions of people watched on television when people first landed on the Moon in 1969.

In 1940 Peter Goldmark **invented** a camera to film television shows in colour. It took until 1954 to make a television set that could show programmes in colour. By the 1970s, most new televisions were colour televisions.

Peter Goldmark was born in Hungary, but moved to the United States.

Cable television

Television **signals** travel through the air. Signals are the picture and sound that make up television shows. At first, people put a television **aerial** on their roof to get the signals. People who lived in the mountains had trouble getting a good television signal.

This man is putting a television aerial on a roof.

A satellite dish helps people who live far away get a good television signal.

Cable television began in the United States in 1948. It made television signals better. **Inventors** worked to find other ways of getting a good television signal. Today people can use an aerial, a cable, or a **satellite dish** to watch television.

Remote control

In 1956 Robert Adler **invented** the first **remote control** for television. The remote turned the TV on and off. It made the TV sound loud or soft. The first remote was **connected** to the TV by a wire. The remote was called "the clicker".

The first remotes had a wire coming out of the bottom.

Today remote controls are easy to use.

By the 1980s, all televisions came with remote controls. Remotes no longer need to be connected to the TV by a wire. People can sit far from the television and change the channels or make the sound louder.

Recording programmes

When television began, people had to watch shows at the time they were **broadcast**, or shown. In 1969 a new system let people record **programmes** to watch later. This system is called a **VCR** (video cassette recorder).

A wire connects a VCR to a television.

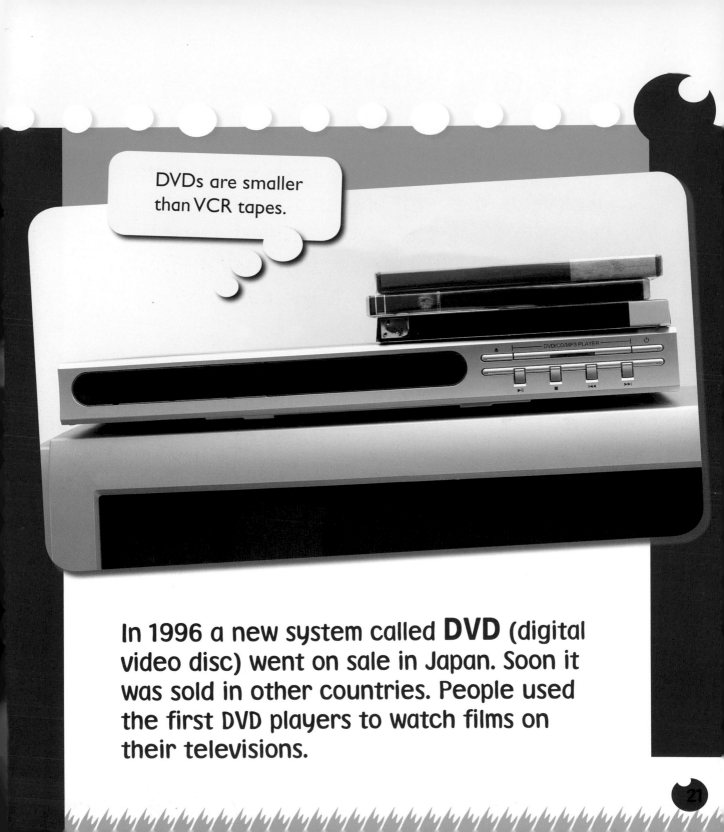

DVDs are smaller than VCR tapes.

In 1996 a new system called **DVD** (digital video disc) went on sale in Japan. Soon it was sold in other countries. People used the first DVD players to watch films on their televisions.

Big TV and web TV

The first TV screens were very small. Over time, they got bigger. In 1993 some televisions had screens that filled a whole wall. People called a room with a giant television a home cinema.

Watching a big TV is almost like going to the cinema.

People need a keyboard to use web TV.

In 1996 **inventors** found a way to use television like a computer to send email and search the **World Wide Web**. They called it **web TV**. Some people did not want to buy a computer, so they used web TV instead.

New kinds of televisions

Inventors continue to make television better. Today new televisions have flat screens. Flat screens take up less room and give a better picture.

Each of these flat-screen TVs is showing a different **programme**.

Some new flat-screen televisions are called **HD** (high-definition) televisions. These televisions can be giant-sized or very tiny. The television picture is better than ever before.

Today televisions have a better picture than ever before.

How television changed life

Today people watch television for fun. People watch **programmes** and films at home. They can watch sports on television while it is happening. People even play video games on the television.

This television camera is filming a race.

Today schools use televisions to help pupils learn.

Today people get the news from television. They can find out what is happening far away by watching television. Children can watch programmes and films on the television to learn. Television has many uses.

Timeline

1924 John Logie Baird **invents** television in the United Kingdom.

1925 Charles Francis Jenkins invents television in the United States.

1927 Philo T. Farnsworth invents an **electronic** television.

1928 First television shows begin.

1940 Peter Goldmark invents colour television.

1948 First **cable service** is tested.

1954 First colour television sets are for sale.

1956 Robert Adler invents **remote control**.

1969 **VCR** is invented.

1993 Big screen televisions are for sale.

1996 First **DVDs** are for sale.

1996 **Web TV** is invented.

1997 First flat-screen televisions are for sale.

World map activity

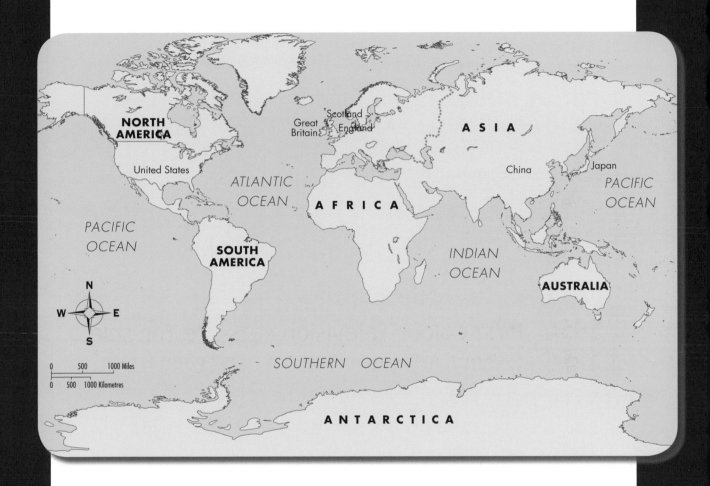

The countries talked about in this book are labelled on this world map. Try to find each **inventor**'s country on the map.

Find out more

Books

In Touch: Television, Chris Oxlade
  (Heinemann Library, 2001).

Inventing the Television, Joanne Richter
  (Crabtree, 2006).

The Television, Marc Tyler Nobleman
  (Fact Finders, 2004).

Websites

Enchanted Learning –
http://www.enchantedlearning.com/inventors

Technology at Home –
http://www.pbs.org/wgbh/aso/tryit/tech

Glossary

aerial wire or set of wires used to receive a television signal

broadcast send through the air to radio or television

cable television system to get better television signals

connect put together

DVD (digital video disc) machine for viewing and recording television shows and movies

electronic something that uses electricity

HD TV (high definition) new kind of television with a better picture

invent make something that didn't exist before

inventor someone who makes something that didn't exist before

programme radio or television show

remote control something that works a television from far away

satellite dish system for getting better television signals

signal sound or picture sent to a television set

theatre place to watch plays

VCR (video cassette recorder) machine for recording and viewing television shows and films

web TV using television to send email or visit websites

World Wide Web (www) computer program that lets people send email and visit websites

Index

Index

Glossary

aerial wire or set of wires used to receive a television signal

broadcast send through the air to radio or television

cable television system to get better television signals

connect put together

DVD (digital video disc) machine for viewing and recording television shows and movies

electronic something that uses electricity

HD TV (high definition) new kind of television with a better picture

invent make something that didn't exist before

inventor someone who makes something that didn't exist before

programme radio or television show

remote control something that works a television from far away

satellite dish system for getting better television signals

signal sound or picture sent to a television set

theatre place to watch plays

VCR (video cassette recorder) machine for recording and viewing television shows and films

web TV using television to send email or visit websites

World Wide Web (www) computer program that lets people send email and visit websites